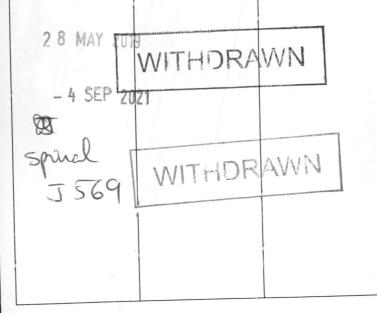

olly
s *Coelodonta*
he snows
g the great
of Earth's
rn lands.

s Books

First published in the UK in 2003 by
(C) Chrysalis Children's Books
an imprint of Chrysalis Books Group Plc
The Chrysalis Building, Bramley Rd,
London W10 6SP

ISBN 1 84138 892 0

British Library Cataloguing in Publication Data
for this book is available from the British Library.

Printed in China
10 9 8 7 6 5 4 3 2 1

Acknowledgements
We wish to thank the following individuals
and organisations for their help and assistance
and for supplying material in their collections:
Alpha Archive: 4 (b), 5 (tr), 6, 7 (tl), 8 (tl), 9,
   10, 11, 12, 13, 18, 19 (br), 20 (tl), 22, 23 (br),
   24 (tl), 27 (br), 29, 30, 32
Corbis Images: 25
Peter Bull Artists: 4 (tl), 7 (b), 15,
Bernard Long: 20 (tl)
Gavin Page: 3
Natural History Museum: 2, 8 (bl), 14, 20 (bl),
   23 (t), 24 (b), 28,
Science Photo Library: 1, 16 (tl), 26 (tl),
John Sibbick: all other illustrations

Editorial Manager: Joyce Bentley
Design and editorial production:
Alpha Communications
Educational advisor: Julie Stapleton
Text editor: Veronica Ross

▲
rh
liv
bo
gla
no

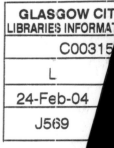

CONTENTS

LOOK FOR THE MAMMOTH BOX

Look for the mammoth logo in boxes like this.
Here you will find extra facts, stories and other
items of interesting information.

FREEZER PLANET

From time to time, the Earth has gone through very cold periods known as ice ages. During each ice age, large parts of the world have been covered in vast sheets of ice.

▲ Woolly rhinoceros once roamed across snowy wastes in Asia.

There have been many ice ages in the Earth's history. The most severe of them turned much of our planet into a chilly snowball for millions of years.

   The most recent ice ages lasted from about 1.6 million years ago to 10 000 years ago. During this time, called the Pleistocene, the ice has come and gone many times and the world's temperature has become warmer or colder. In the cold spells, much of the northern half of our world was frozen under layers of ice hundreds of metres deep.

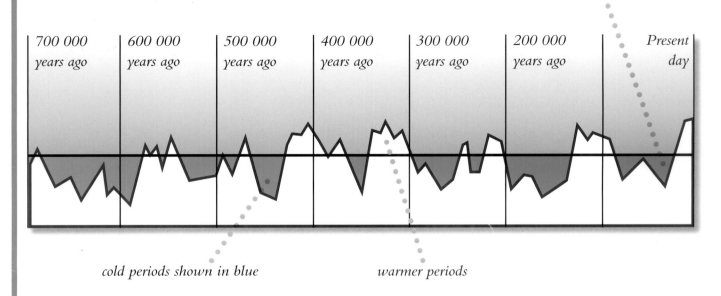

coldest part of last ice age, 18-20 000 years ago

| 700 000 years ago | 600 000 years ago | 500 000 years ago | 400 000 years ago | 300 000 years ago | 200 000 years ago | Present day |

cold periods shown in blue   *warmer periods*

▲ There have been several ice ages in the last 700 000 years, when temperatures dropped.

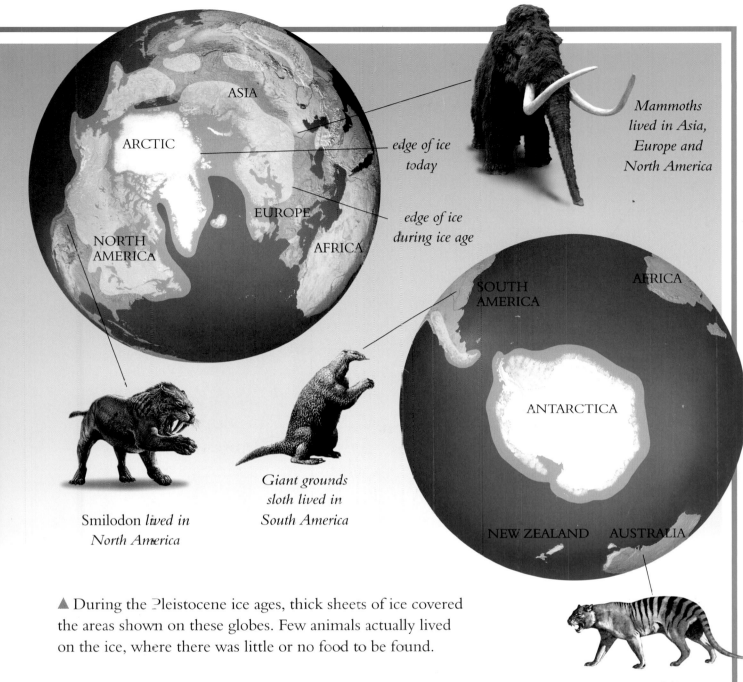

Mammoths
lived in Asia,
Europe and
North America

edge of ice
today

edge of ice
during ice age

Smilodon *lived in
North America*

*Giant grounds
sloth lived in
South America*

*Marsupial lions
lived in Australia*

▲ During the Pleistocene ice ages, thick sheets of ice covered
the areas shown on these globes. Few animals actually lived
on the ice, where there was little or no food to be found.

During the coldest parts of the Pleistocene ice ages almost
one-third of the Earth's land area was covered with ice.
Some of the animals that lived then were familiar-looking
creatures, such as wolves and bears. But others were
strange-looking beasts, unlike animals living today.

Ice still covers large areas around the North and South
Poles, as well as high mountains. We live in a warmer time
at present, but there may be another ice age in the future.

ICY BLANKET

As temperatures dropped, so ice sheets advanced into places that had been warmer, grinding their way over the landscape at up to a metre per day.

glacier more than 1.6 km thick

During the Pleistocene ice ages, huge glaciers and vast ice sheets covered much of North America, Europe and Asia, as well as covering Antarctica completely. The ice could be very thick. Wide areas were covered with layers of packed ice, more than 1.6 km deep.

Animals in the cold zones had a daily battle to survive. Many plants were buried in snow, making it difficult for plant-eating animals to find food. Many animals grew thick, shaggy coats for warmth in the freezing conditions.

◄ The world's tallest office buildings are presently the Petronas Towers in Malaysia. But big as they are, these 452m-high structures are tiny compared to many ice age glaciers.

Petronas Towers

During ice age summers, temperatures became a little warmer and some ice melted from the glaciers. Water from the melting ice became chilly streams that gushed across the land. The flowing water helped plants grow again, so animals could find more to eat.

WHAT IS A GLACIER?

A glacier is a river of ice that moves slowly downhill, grinding away anything that stands in the way. Soil, rocks and entire landscapes can be crushed by the moving ice. The top of a glacier may be covered in fresh snow, but as the snow builds up, its weight squashes the layers below to form a solid mass of heavy ice.

There are many glaciers today, but they are formed only near the poles and in high mountain areas – the one pictured here is in the Canadian Rocky Mountains.

▼ This is how an ice age glacier may have looked at its foot, or lowest point. The ice dumps a constant supply of water, rocks and gravel.

running streams and waterfalls caused by melting ice

mammoths ate grass and other vegetation

CAVE CREATURES

Many animals escaped the icy chill by moving to warmer lands. Other animals used caves as shelter during the long, cold winters.

▲ A glacier scraped out this rugged cliff at Creswell Crags in Britain. The caves were used by many animals over the years.

One of the cave-dwelling animals was the 2m-long cave bear, *Ursus spelaeus*. This big bear lived across much of Europe during the Pleistocene, escaping the worst of the deep freeze by sleeping through the winter in caves. Researchers have found a large cave in Austria littered with the bones of dead bears. It seems that lots of bears shared the cave, but a few died each winter. Over thousands of years the cave turned into a huge bears' graveyard.

The cave lion *Panthera leo spelaea* was another animal that sheltered in caves. It grew up to about 3.5 m long, about one quarter bigger than lions today and lived in Europe as far north as Denmark, until about 2000 years ago.

◄ Cave bears have not survived to the present day. They were common in Europe throughout the Pleistocene ice ages.

Hyenas were hunting animals that used caves as dens during the last ice age. Caves provided safe shelter for pups and freshly-killed animals could be dragged to the safety of the cave to eat. Remains show that ice age hyenas hunted mostly bison, plus a few horses and reindeer.

▲ Until about 20 000 years ago, hyenas lived in much of Europe. They hunted in packs and also ate scraps left by other predators. Today hyenas live only in Africa.

EARLY HUMAN HUNTERS

Scientists think that early human tribes survived through many ice age periods. Humans often used caves as homes and chased many different animals for food and for their skins. Tribal artists decorated the walls of their caves in France and Spain. These paintings feature hunting scenes that show mammoth and bison. People also learned to store meat rather than having to eat a whole carcass in one sitting. In summer, the meat was dried, in winter it was left to freeze in the snow. The frozen meat could be cooked later over a roaring fire.

HAIRY GIANT

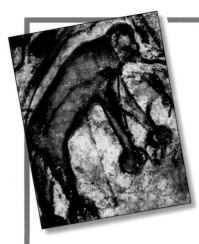

The mammoth is probably the best-known ice age animal. This huge beast had a thick, hairy coat that protected it from the bitter cold.

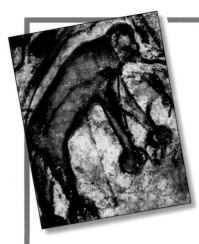

▲ Early humans often decorated their caves with paintings of mammoths. Most of the paintings have been found in caves in France and Spain. The art is thought to be about 30 000 years old.

Mammoths lived across much of North America, Europe and Asia. Adults could grow more than 3m tall and spent their lives in herds, wandering through woods and grasslands, eating the plants that grew there.

There were several kinds of mammoth, but not all of them lived in snow zones. For example, the imperial mammoth lived farther south and grew about 4m high.

The earliest mammoths appeared about 2 million years ago. But a few may have survived to much more recent times. Some remains found on a Siberian island may be only about 4000 years old.

◀ Apart from humans, wolves were the only enemy a mammoth faced. A pack of hungry wolves could chase and eventually bring down a sick or injured mammoth.

adult mammoth had a domed head and a shoulder hump

▶ Woolly mammoths had shaggy hair that could grow nearly 1m long. The mammoth used its trunk for feeling and grasping things, similar to the way we use our hands.

CURVING TUSKS

Mammoths had two huge, curving tusks that sometimes grew so long that they crossed over each other. Males used their tusks at mating time to fight each other over females. They were also useful for sweeping aside snow to get at buried food.

BODY IN THE ICE

trunk grew about 2m long

the biggest mammoths weighed up to 10 tonnes

mammoth ate up to 225 kg of food a day, mostly grass

We know more about ice age beasts than earlier creatures such as the dinosaurs. This is because remains of their bodies have been found frozen in ice.

▲ Under their skin, mammoths had a layer of fat up to 10 cm thick.

SIBERIA

the young mammoth called Dima was found here

Although we do not live in an ice age at present, northern Siberia remains very cold, and much of the land stays frozen all year round to a depth of 500m. Even in summer, only the top few metres thaw out.

It was here that a young male mammoth was found by miners digging for gold in 1977. The miners were using bulldozers to clear away frozen soil, and this is how the mammoth was discovered. When it died the animal was only about nine months old. One autumn day it had slipped and drowned in a deep mud pool. When winter came, the body was frozen solid.

▲ The young mammoth found in Siberia was called Dima after a nearby stream.

WHAT'S IN A NAME?

The word mammoth comes from a very old Siberian word *mammot* meaning 'earth burrower'. Instead of being an animal from the past, the mammoth was thought to be a giant underground beast, rather like a huge mole. People believed that when an earth burrower came to the surface, it died in the open air. This explained why only remains were found, instead of living animals.

The mammoth, named Dima, was less than 1m high and still had its first set of teeth, the first of six sets that mammoths grew during their lives.

Dima died about 40 000 years ago, but scientists managed to find traces of the last meal – grass – that lay in its stomach. Other ice age beasts have been dug up, but Dima's is the most complete body that has been found.

HORNED BEASTS

There were several kinds of ice age rhinoceros. The biggest of them weighed nearly four tonnes and had a huge horn growing out of its forehead.

The 6m-long *Elasmotherium* lived in Europe and Asia during the Pleistocene ice age until only about 10 000 years ago.

The *Elasmotherium*'s horn was made of the same sort of hard material as your fingernails. Experts believe it grew up to 2m long.

▲ Like all rhinos, the *Elasmotherium* was a plant-eater, surviving on a mixture of grasses, twigs, shoots and leaves.

The woolly rhino *Coelodonta* was smaller than the *Elasmotherium*, and had a thick, hairy coat for warmth with two large, curving horns on its head.

Today's rhinoceros is known for its short sight and for being easily startled. The woolly rhino was probably similar. In a fight, its huge front horn would have made a good weapon to sweep aside other animals. The horn could also have been used to shovel snow from side to side, so the plant-eating woolly rhino could reach grass growing under the snow.

ARE THEY CLAWS OR HORNS?

Many remains of woolly rhinos have been found, especially in northern Russia where their bodies were frozen solid in the icy soil of Siberia. Remains were first found in the nineteenth century, but at first researchers thought the strange, curving horn was the claw of a giant prehistoric bird. More recent discoveries include some 30 000-year-old rhino skeletons dug up in a British quarry in 2002. The skeletons were found with those of other ice age animals and some plants that looked as if they had been buried only a few weeks! Today there are five kinds of rhinoceros: two in Africa, three in Asia. The Sumatran rhino is the closest surviving relative.

woolly rhino had a big hump over its shoulders

front horn curved like a sword blade

▼ An adult woolly rhino weighed over 2 tonnes. These animals lived in many parts of Europe and Asia.

SABRE TOOTH!

Sabre-tooth cats were named after their huge, front teeth shaped like a curved sword, called a sabre. There were several different kinds of these ferocious animals.

▶ Many prehistoric animals were preserved after they fell into the sticky La Brea tar pits in California, USA. Here a *Smilodon* feasts on a dead body before it sinks into the tar.

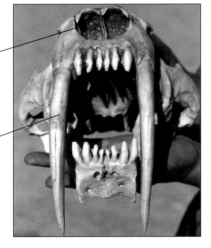

nostril holes

sabre tooth

◀ *Smilodon* had jaws that opened very wide to allow its huge teeth to strike at prey.

Sabre-tooth cats lived from more than 5 million years ago to about 10 000 years ago. Various kinds lived in North and South America, Africa, Europe and Asia – and one of the biggest was the *Smilodon*. It grew nearly 3m long, larger than today's tiger. *Smilodon* had powerful front legs and shoulders, which allowed it to wrestle animals to the ground easily.

Sabre-tooth cats had very sharp teeth, but they chipped easily if the cat bit too hard on bone. The teeth were brittle, too, and could snap if prey twisted strongly. So a *Smilodon* aimed to kill with one swift bite to the soft parts of its prey's neck. The cat's jaws opened extra-wide to allow its 25 cm-long fangs a quick, deep, slicing thrust.

Smilodon

FIGHTING FOR SURVIVAL

Smilodon was larger than a present-day tiger
and one of the fiercest prehistoric hunting
animals. But these big cats did not have it all
their own way – many prey animals fought
back strongly. Many *Smilodon* remains show
minor injuries (such as broken teeth) while
other remains show more serious injuries,
including broken hip bones and jaws.

HUGE ANTLERS

The *Megaloceros* was a big Pleistocene deer that lived through the ice ages, from about 400 000 years ago until less than 10 000 years ago.

▲ The first antlered deer was the *Dicrocerus* of 7 million years ago.

The male *Megaloceros* had the biggest antlers of any deer that has ever lived. A full-grown adult was nearly 3m tall, and its antlers could grow more than 3m across.

◀ Only the male *Megaloceros* had huge antlers. These large deer lived in most of Europe and parts of central Asia.

a big male weighed up to 700 kg

A male *Megaloceros* grew a new set of antlers each year. The growing season lasted about four months and during this time the antlers grew more than 8 mm every day. To fuel this growth, a *Megaloceros* had to eat about 40 kg of grass and twigs daily, also nibbling at springtime willow tree shoots. The willow provided minerals (such as calcium) which were needed to give the antlers strength.

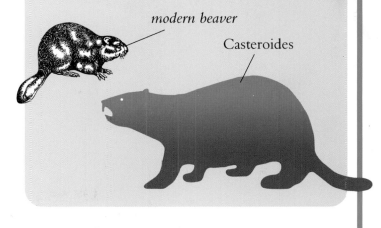

3.6m

1.7m

◄ Scientists have found remains of *Megaloceros* that are only 9200 years old. These recent survivors may have been hunted by early human tribes.

A full set of tough antlers was needed in late August. For this time of year was when the male *Megaloceros* used their antlers for display and to fight each other to see which animal could mate with the female deer.

Strength was needed for the many fights that followed. These were very tiring, even for a big stag with antlers weighing up to 40 kg.

After mating, males and females lived apart. Soon the huge antlers fell off, to be replaced by a new set that started growing the following spring.

BIG BEAVER

In North America, a giant beaver called the *Casteroides* lived among the lakes and forests. An adult *Casteroides* had a scaly tail, 15-cm long cutting teeth and grew up to 2.5m long. It weighed about 200 kg, seven times more than a 30 kg beaver of today.

modern beaver

Casteroides

SOUTHERN GIANTS

Macrauchenia *grew over 2m at the shoulder*

▲ Huge herds of *Macrauchenia* lived on grassy plains until 10 000 years ago.

While much of the north was frozen during the Pleistocene, most of South America was much warmer. It had lots of its own animal species.

South America was once an island. It joined with North America about 3 to 4 million years ago. Until then South America's animals had developed separately and there were many strange beasts that lived nowhere else.

For example the camel-sized *Macrauchenia* had a short trunk, like that of a modern tapir. The *Megatherium* was a huge ground sloth that weighed up to 3 tonnes.

◄ Giant ground sloths used their tail as a useful prop when plucking leaves from trees. The *Megatherium* was the biggest sloth, growing up to 6m long. It was the biggest sloth ever known and today's sloths that hang from the branches of trees are its distant relatives.

Glyptodonts were South America's living tanks, having thick armour to protect them. Glyptodonts came in various sizes, but the biggest was the *Doedicurus*, which grew up to 3m long and weighed more than a tonne. It was the ancestor of the modern armadillo, a much smaller animal.

For a hungry predator, killing any glyptodont was quite a challenge. The body was covered in a tough shell of six-sided scales (called scutes), and some kinds had an armoured tail that ended in a 40-kg spiked ball. One hit from this and any soft-skinned animal would have been injured or killed.

▲ Predators attack a glyptodont. They stand a good chance of bringing it down by working in a team, rather than working singly.

WALKING TO A NEW WORLD

It seems odd to think of continents moving – but they do, although very slowly. North and South America joined together at a narrow neck of land called the Isthmus of Panama. After this happened, animals from both sides could walk to new lands. North American animals that moved south included mice, squirrels, bears and wolves. Going north were animals such as opossums, sloths and armadillos. Not all these creatures survived in their new homes – giant ground sloths died out in North America a few thousand years ago. But the armadillo is still spreading across Texas and other southern states of the USA.

Isthmus of Panama

LIFE DOWN UNDER

▲ The *Thylacoleo* lion (top) weighed up to 130 kg. The *Diprotodon* weighed more than 2 tonnes.

Australia and New Zealand mostly escaped the great ice sheets of the Pleistocene. Animals that lived in Australia included giant wombats, while huge birds lived in New Zealand.

The mammals of Pleistocene Australia were all marsupials. These are animals that carry and feed their young in a pouch. The biggest marsupial of all was the *Diprotodon*, a large wombat the size of a modern hippopotamus. *Diprotodon* was a plant-eater. Remains of these creatures have been found in deep mud where they were trapped trying to reach tasty vegetation.

The *Thylacoleo* was a giant marsupial lion with deadly front teeth and claws that could snap in and out of its paws. The first complete skeleton was found in a cave in Western Australia in 2002. The bones are thought to have been there for about 1.5 million years.

 ALIVE OR EXTINCT?

Until a few thousand years ago, the dog-like *Thylacinus* was common in Australia. *Thylacinus* could run steadily over long distances, chasing prey until it was exhausted and could be killed easily. The last-known Tasmanian wolf, a later and smaller version of *Thylacinus*, died in a zoo in 1936. But there are sometimes reports of odd survivors living in remote areas.

stripes only on rear half of body

◄ The 200 kg *Procoptodon* could hop along at more than 50 km/h.

The biggest marsupial today is the red kangaroo. It grows about 1.5m tall, but its ancestor was another Pleistocene giant, the *Procoptodon*. This was a 'mega-roo' that was twice as big as the red kangaroo. Despite their size, *Procoptodons* probably lived much like kangaroos do now, living in groups, hopping around to feed on grass and bushes.

New Zealand's biggest animals were birds. The moa was a huge, flightless bird that weighed as much as a pony and grew over 3m tall. Today, moas are extinct – humans killed the last of them only a few hundred years ago.

▼ The moa laid giant eggs measuring up to 20 cm across.

A WARMER WORLD

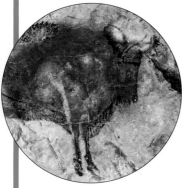

▲ Experts think this cave painting of a bison was made about 20 000 years ago.

The last ice age ended about 10 000 years ago when most of the great ice sheets melted. Since then we have been living in warmer times.

When the last ice age ended, life became easier for many animals. However, latest research shows that the great warm-up was not a slow event – the climate probably changed in less than a century. This was too fast for some kinds of animal to adjust. Ice age giants such as the woolly rhino and almost all mammoths died out.

Ice age humans probably helped kill off some species, too. Cave paintings show spear-equipped hunters chasing mammoth, deer and bison.

▲ The Aurochs was a huge ox that had horns up to 4m across and weighed more than a tonne.

▲ Humans were deadly hunters. Even the biggest animal had little defence against a group of humans attacking with sharp spears.

Today, many scientists are more worried about the Earth getting too hot than the world plunging into another ice age. Pollution from human activities seems to be slowly raising temperatures on our planet.

Recent studies have shown that the ice cap covering the North Pole is much thinner than it was in 1970. If the world carries on warming at its present rate, then the ice cap could melt completely by the year 2080, leaving open sea in its place.

FAREWELL ICE CAPS?

Could cold-loving animals survive if the ice melted at the Earth's poles? It would be easier for some than for others. Animals such as polar bears would be very badly affected by melting ice. The Arctic ice cap floats on open sea, so large parts of the polar bear's habitat would turn to water.

Humans would be big losers if the ice on Antarctica melted. Sea levels around the world would rise and thousands of coastal towns and cities would be flooded.

ICE AGE BEASTS WORDS

Here are some technical terms used in this book.

▲ A woolly rhino's skull, showing the two huge horns.

antler
The branched horns of a deer. They fall off in autumn and grow back the following year.

armoured
Thick skin grown by some animals. Glyptodonts in South America had scales that protected them from predators.

climate
A general word that describes the long-term weather patterns of a place or region.

continent
One of Earth's main land masses – Africa, Asia, Europe, North and South America, Antarctica and Oceania, which includes Australia, New Zealand and small islands.

extinct
An animal or plant species that has died out.

glacier
A huge mass of ice that moves slowly downhill like a river of ice. Glaciers often make valleys by grinding away rock and soil.

isthmus
A narrow neck of land that joins two larger areas of land. The Isthmus of Panama joins North and South America.

land bridge
A shallow part of the sea floor that becomes dry land if the sea level drops, joining places that were once separated by water. During the Pleistocene, huge amounts of sea water were frozen as ice, and sea levels fell hundreds of metres.

mammal
A warm-blooded animal, such as a bear or human. Mammals normally have fur or hair and babies feed on mother's milk.

marsupial
A type of mammal that has a pouch in which its babies are kept while they feed on their mother's milk.

mineral
A non-living material that occurs naturally in the earth, many of which are essential to life. For example, the mineral calcium is needed for bones to grow and be strong.

Pleistocene

The period of time from 1.6 million years ago to 10 000 years ago, during which the Earth was going through its last series of ice ages.

poles

The coldest parts of the Earth, at the north and south of the planet. Both poles are covered with permanent ice caps.

pollution

Harmful waste, such as exhaust fumes from vehicles, released into the environment.

prey

An animal that is hunted by another animal for food.

species

A group of living things that can breed among themselves, and have young that can also do the same.

tar pit

A lake of sticky black liquid, formed when crude oil seeps to the surface through cracks in rocks below ground.

WEIRD WORDS

This pronunciation guide will help you say the ice age words in this book.

Aurochs
or-rox

Casteroides
cass-ter-oy-deez

Coelodonta
see-low-don-ta

Dicrocerus
dik-ross-er-us

Diprotodon
dip-rot-oh-don

Doedicurus
dee-dick-er-us

Elasmotherium
all-az-moh-theer-ee-um

Glyptodont
glip-toe-dont

Hyena
high-ee-na

Macrauchenia
mack-ror-cheen-ee-ar

Megaloceros
mega-loss-er-oss

Megatherium
mega-theer-ree-um

Panthera leo spelaea
pan-thair-ra lee-oh spel-aye-ah

Pleistocene
ply-stoh-seen

Procoptodon
pro-kop-ter-don

Rhinoceros
rye-noss-er-uss

Siberia
sigh-beer ree-ah

Smilodon
smil-er-don

Thylacinus
thil-ack-in-us

Thylacoleo
thil-ack-oh-lee-oh

Ursus spelaeus
er-suss spel-aye-uss

six-sided scales are called scutes

◄ Remains of a glyptodon, showing its armoured body.

ICE AGE BEASTS FACTS

Here are some facts and stories about the ice age world.

Many ice ages

Researchers have evidence for at least 20 ice ages, stretching back millions of years. Ideas to explain them range from wobbles in the Earth's path around the Sun to times when we are surrounded by space dust. Events like these reduce the heat Earth receives from the Sun. A drop of just a few degrees is all it takes to plunge the Earth into an ice age.

Bridge across the water

So much seawater was frozen during the ice ages that ocean levels fell many metres. Places that had been sea bed became dry and formed 'land bridges' whch lasted for thousands of years. For example, Britain was once joined to Europe, and North America was joined to Asia. Many animals and people of early human tribes crossed land bridges to new places.

Museum monsters

Dinosaurs are usually more popular than ice age beasts, but it wasn't always so. In early Victorian times, no dinosaurs had yet been found. Ice age animals were the oldest creatures thought to exist. In fact, most people thought that the Earth was just 6000 years old, instead of the 4.5 billion years presently estimated.

Tusk traders

There was once a big trade in mammoth tusks. The ivory

◄ The prehistoric North American bison was bigger than today's animal, and lived in smaller herds. It had much longer horns.

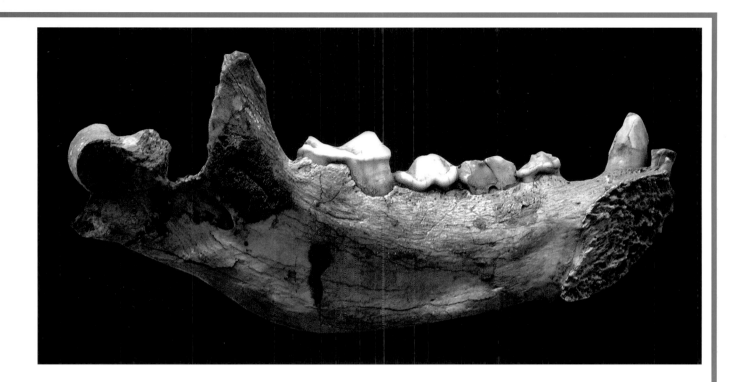

was carved into works of art and items such as combs. In the early twentieth century tusks from more than 200 mammoths – a total weight of about 20 tonnes – were sold each year in Siberian markets. Mammoth tusks are still valuable and a tusk in good condition can be worth $1000.

Tasty mammoth

From time to time, frozen mammoth remains are found in perfect condition. In the past, a few people have actually eaten thawed-out mammoth flesh, and others have fed the meat to their dogs. Today, things are different and mammoth remains are highly valued for science research – a complete mammoth can be worth $1 million or more.

Elk from Ireland?

The *Megaloceros* is also called the 'Irish elk', because remains were first found in an Irish peat bog. But it was not an elk nor was it only from Ireland. *Megaloceros* was a type of deer and it lived all over Europe.

Big baby

A newly born mammoth weighed about 90 kg, growing to about 9-10 tonnes when adult. Most human babies weigh only 2.5-4 kg at birth.

▲ This jawbone of a cave bear was found in Europe. Bears used the cave as a safe place for their winter sleep.

Tar pit treasures

The tar pits at La Brea in California have preserved a treasure trove of prehistoric animals, including mammoth, bison, sabre-tooth cats and many others. About one million bones have been found so far. Some bones date back 8000 years, others are more than 40 000 years old.

ICE AGE BEASTS SUMMARY

From time to time, the Earth goes through very cold periods, called ice ages. During an ice age, glaciers cover large parts of our planet.

The last ice age was at its coldest 18-20 000 years ago, in a time called the Pleistocene. Almost one-third of the land was covered in ice and snow. The best-known ice age beast is the woolly mammoth, which had a thick hairy coat to keep it warm. Other animals living at this time included woolly rhinos and sabre-tooth cats. Many lands in the north were frozen but South America and Australia were not. Animals that lived there did not need to survive very cold winters. The world has warmed up since the ice age, and many ice-age beasts have since died out.

▼ Some museums have displays that show ice age animals. Here a giant sloth's skeleton reaches right up to the roof.

ICE AGE BEASTS ON THE WEB

You can find information about ice age beasts on the Internet. Use a search engine and type in the name of the animal you want to find out about. Here are some good sites to start with:

▼ Here are some screenshots from websites that show ice age beasts.

http://www.bbc.co.uk/beasts

This site is based on the information presented in the acclaimed TV series *Walking with Beasts*. The huge website is jam-packed with facts, and includes details of several ice age animals.

http://www.creswell-crags.org.uk

A website that gives lots of information about a fascinating visitor centre in Britain. It is a steep-sided gorge that was carved out by the grinding weight of slow-moving glaciers.

http://www.nature.ca/notebooks/english/icevan.htm

Most of Canada was buried in ice and this site shows many of the animals that survived in the chilly conditions of Vancouver Island.

http://www.mammothsite.com

The Mammoth Hot Springs in South Dakota, USA, are the focus for this site. It is packed with photos and research information. There are also details of entry fees and opening hours.

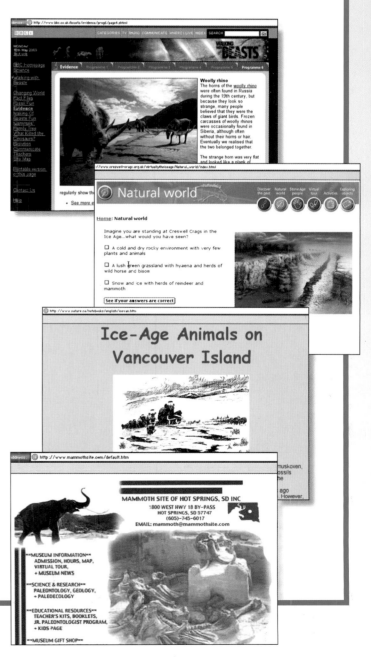